Double Going

Double Going

Poems by

RICHARD FOERSTER

AMERICAN POETS CONTINUUM SERIES, NO. 70

BOA Editions, Ltd. — Rochester, NY — 2002

First Edition
02 03 04 05   7 6 5 4 3 2 1

Publications by BOA Editions, Ltd.—
a not-for-profit corporation under section 501 (c) (3)
of the United States Internal Revenue Code—
are made possible with the assistance of grants from
the Literature Program of the New York State Council on the Arts,
the Literature Program of the National Endowment for the Arts,
the Lannan Foundation, the Sonia Raiziss Giop Charitable Foundation,
the Chase Manhattan Foundation, the CIRE Foundation, Citibank,
as well as from the Mary S. Mulligan Charitable Trust,
the County of Monroe, NY,
and from many individual supporters.

Cover Design: Geri McCormick
Cover Art: "The Crying Man Comforted by Himself at Ten Years of Age" by DeLoss
    McGraw, 1996. Gouache on Paper, 30" x 22". Collection of the author.
Manufacturing: McNaughton & Gunn, Lithographers
BOA Logo: Mirko

Library of Congress Cataloging-in-Publication Data

Foerster, Richard, 1949–
    Double going / Richard Foerster.
        p. cm. -- (American poets continuum series ; no. 70)
    ISBN 1–929918–17–8 (pbk. : alk. paper)
    I. Title. II. Series.

    PS3556.O23 D68 2002
    811'.54--dc21   2001035505

BOA Editions, Ltd.
Steven Huff, Publisher
Richard Garth, Chair
A. Poulin, Jr., President & Founder (1976–1996)
260 East Avenue
Rochester, NY 14604

www.boaeditions.org

State of the Arts

NYSCA

NATIONAL
ENDOWMENT
FOR THE ARTS

for my sisters
Loretta Casey & Harriet Maldonado

CONTENTS

I. Velocities of the Lost

II. The Knot

III. Retrievals

Double Going

I. Velocities of the Lost

Go away go away my rainbow
Charming colors go
For you this exile's essential
        —Apollinaire

THE LOST

At some point you begin to wonder where
things lost in childhood have gone,

how they become the dark matter
inexplicably accounting for more

than the shimmering weight of galaxies,
—how an aggie, for example, whose light

long ago slipped beyond reach, as if
through a black hole in a pocket,

can gather again its critical mass
in the mind till it flashes out from that abyss,

a beacon deep within a space
you never manage to fathom, —or how

a tattered bear that one thought he'd clutch
tighter than any flesh, though even then

milk-sour and button-blind, still seems to be
racing off, perfect on its solitary journey,

deeper through an endless tunnel, yet gesturing
faintly back to the child it left sundered

on a subway platform. Time's relative
when you calculate velocities of the lost, moving

through their vast distances, always away from
yet always toward no destination.

———

PHOTOGRAPH OF ANGELA, 1929

The roadster my mother's sister leans against,
somewhere along the South Jersey shore,
any bootlegger could afford, its hood
coffin-long, its running board wide enough
to support the petite strapped pump
of her left foot. She's eased back
to jut her chin directly toward the sun,
flapper smart, in a cloche from which
just two tight curls ring out, but the way
her calf, her knee, the hint of thigh
are angled for whatever man
framed her there in his lens

was a pose my mother so despised
half a century later that she let me keep
this one print from the trove we found
in Angela's prison-barred Miami home.
The snapshot still smelled of her death
and the bleach that neighbors used to disinfect
the tiles where her corpse had drained
from sofa to floor, but when I showed
my father, asking if he knew where
the photo was shot, "damn" was all he said
at first, then smiled—and from the corner
of my eye, I saw my mother wince.

—

A BRIEF SURVEY OF NEUROLOGY

1.   Petit Mal

This is how, perhaps,
we first came to know
the gods: tiny ailment,

a sudden advent of dread,
and more dread in the shuddering
wake: how the mind winged

open to the unforeseen
dimension, the chaotic prime,
stirred brew of all

we ever were: we
could not live there, could
not bear to have the world's

remnants we had stitched
into a coat of lights
ripped, then remade again

and again: yet here's this
swaddling aura, this nimbus
we're stunned each time to wear.

2. Tourette's

the curse // he cannot cut
the electric sizzle // from his brain
the sputter // spark // the arcing
overload of words // or splice
the frayed cord // to make his syntax
hum // flickofaswitch // on off // off
on // he never knows which //
or if // or when // speech jabs him
// day // night // fricative scat //
jismed jazz // language the stick
// his head the rattled cage

3. Grand Mal

Newtonian decay. A narrowing ellipse.
A comet's detonation plunging through

the upper atmospheres: below, the plane
geometry of life, scorched and curling

at the borders; letters lifting from the glorious
page; all the strata of being in evaporate blaze.

Synaptic nest. What breed of phoenix is this,
what ashen wings stirring in the afterflame?

—

THE WEIGHT OF THE PAST

My blood never seemed as thick
as the dark and bitter Bavarian ale
the Carmelites brewed in their barley-sour
vaults beneath his village church.
Time and again growing up, through long
Sunday afternoons in my father's
favorite saloon in the Bronx, I'd hear
him praise to heaven the not-forgotten
friars' art as he hoisted the thinner,
9-karat lights of his Rhein-
gold beers—*American piss!*
he'd spit—but drink it nonetheless
to his dying day. Tight in his sullen
grip, I staggered through my boyhood
beside him, back to the waiting cold
suppers, early baths, and then
recrimination's rages seeping
beneath my cracked bedroom door.
Once, as if to untap the hidden
spring of my father's drinking, or
perhaps to notch him down a peg,
my mother told of his killing a boy
my age—how the heavy Daimler
limousine he drove at twenty
swerved on ice on Christmas Eve,
crushing the child against a wall.
I never asked my father where
or why. I had no need for facts.
The truth my mother divulged—or fiction—
pressed down like an executioner's stone.

—

THE LIGHTHOUSE AT CASSIS

Verdant light, yours is the fallacy
of concern, its pulse and spin

projected far from this harbored
calm, sign to any eye sea-sliced

at the dimensionless edge that a vessel's
every rigging is wind-wail at the end.

I'd rather not have your unsettling
glare tonight outside the room where I sit

adrift on this foam of words, this tidal
monotony eddying feebly about your base.

The facts are he jumped from a bridge,
his soul having drowned long before

his body did, and I cannot cry for him,
my sister's son. Instead I clutch at this elegy

like a tissue, a prop in a posture of grief.
And yet I'd like to think whatever beacon

flashed as he stood wavering over the black
Pacific, its light skittering across the water—

as now, here, for me, setting fireflies pulsing green-
gold in the waves—should have been enough

to dazzle him back to this world. But how that illusion,
like these words, can merely play atop a grave.

—

TANTUM ERGO

What here redeems us? Surely
not this posture of reverence
before the tabernacle's hasp

pinned into place, nor that
tiny burnished door, secure
beneath a candleflame. The cosmic

burst when finally it hinges
open—the host removed—
leaves the all-too-ponderable

space: another empty tomb.
And now the monstrance
blinds almost beyond reason

while voices accede to Aquinas'
hymn amid heady swirls
of frankincense and organ swell,

the aggrieved bones' reverberations;
each sense amens even
to the brink—but then this

undersong throbs through
the temples, its insistent
Miserere laps like a tide.

—

PEONIES

—not fists, for that implies
           something willed, stunned
rage, the obstinate child's
      held breath, his flush in-
fusions of color that
           would stay clamped, not
burst, but insist even
      as the sepals split,
flutter down, modesty's
           garb, exposing
the cause, a plaint: all bruise

—which now dark agents lick,
      like ants scouring
for some nourishment there,
      peeling each petal
back as if it were un-
      natural, this
unrestrained unfolding
      to become what must
strain under its own weight
      not to topple
and then, in full cry, must.

for Carl Phillips

ANNA'S HOUSE

Bad Neustadt, 1956

My father's sister's Unterfranken Deutsch
my mother called "peasantish." All through
that summer visit, I watched my aunt for signs

and listened from deep inside the near-
empty cave of my Bronx-bred English.
Ignorant, by half, of everything around me,

I didn't understand what I feared: the black
sweep of curtain-heavy skirts as she went,
stiff as a broom, about her chores;

or the greens she'd boil dark as hemlock,
her kitchen's bitter steam as she tonged
the limp mass from a bubbling iron pot

and spread it on the block; the broad blade
then firmly in her hands, shuddering,
thrumming it toward a thin—what?

Mix it with potatoes, Anna, for the boy . . .
something he knows, my mother urged
in High German tones. By the nods

I knew, and by the wooden spoon's insistent
gesturing toward my lips, as if to say
Schmekt gut. But struggling against a gag,

my throat clamped round its own gutturals
in vain attempts to keep the spinach down.
And all that summer I feared the red shutters

she'd snap to spell an end to my lingering
dusks and bring unearthly glooms to the bed
where I'd be sent to pout and finally sleep.

And yet, one dawn, I braved sneaking out
from beside my mother and found Anna
by the stove, hard-stroking the gray

waist-length veil of her hair, and watched
in silence the deft practice of her fingers
blindly braiding it until, arms upraised,

as if caught in the slow grace of an ancient
patterned dance, she swirled the long
twinned snake of hair three times

about her head and with one sure thrust
of a pin fixed it in a tight constraint.
Afraid she'd catch me spying, I crept back

beside my mother's frame. Decades later
the boy I was still sleeps somewhere inside
that house; his fear was the dream I now fear

waking from.

———

INSECTS AT NIGHT

. . . and the grasshopper shall be a burden . . .
—Ecclesiastes 12:5

Why this trembling at the cicada's tremolo,
at the studded black beyond the screen, why

this scuttling heart? I arc at every flutter.
Such wayward urgency afflicts the dark—

like scraps of a torn-up letter—such relentless
pulsing toward available light, a pallor

of prayers winging toward the splintered moon.
The oiled dust of their generations covers

my house. I've become a rattle of charnel
bones invaded by beetles, the tapping deep

inside the bed, the pillow thrumming a Morse
I understand too well. The cecropia's eyes

are zeroes; the mantis, a prophetess of want.
The caravans of wood lice seek only

a rotting world. Revenant cells, not souls.
O troubled void. Delusion of sleep. What

mantra must I make the crickets chirr
beyond their answering *repeat*? A method

only, then. A bending, a forging link
by link: enchaining toward some infinite.

WISTERIA

Years I let the wisteria run, hoping
in abandon that the double-twisted vines
which climbed the sugar maples would bloom and fill
each April's leafless air with pale-grape clusters,
with bee-hum infusions after long winter.
What began as young ribbon snakes coiling up
along a few limbs grew Hydralike, the trunk
anaconda thick, each new season's tendrils
lushly green and rivaling the maples' own:
like lovers entwined in one another's flesh,
but flowerless, lavish in the lack. July,
I'd prune what I could reach—the buggy-whip shoots,
pinnate switches interlaced like healers' wands—
yet in fall among the trees' crimson, a fool's
bounty of gold would shower down and I'd see
against the frigid sky the years' contorted
increments: How many summers did I press
lips to nipples, let my fingers idly twine
the wet coarse hair, sweat with arousal, wanting,
if not the genes' imperative, then the thrust
and brief florescence?—a childless present tense.

—

FOG

York Beach, Maine

Gauze of morning, the hidden
world: a wound, a throb
somewhere, nowhere palpably
near. What I want's unfocused:
a stolid opposite house—
Calvinist, shuttered black;
the clapboarded white—not this

spume, not this thought-
free gull winging into mist,
and gone, the once chiseled
forms unsculpted, back
to pure Carrara, the captive
eye rolled up inside
its socket: this epileptic

sky, this dull tin-
tinnabulum, skull-deep,
phonemic, clapped, and fused.
O God, ravel me out,
let me see the merest
cinder burning through
the shroud, then . . . conflagration.

———

CHURCH BURNING

Already it is almost nothing, a darkness
settled beneath a dusting of stars.
An after-hiss. A braiding of ghosts.

For someone has imagined himself
watching from a crowd, staggered
along a dirt road in Georgia.

On that night he will be as he is now:
a silhouette pasted against the glare,
a cipher, an absence intermingling.

For already the steeple has collapsed
with the thunder of a single word,
and the bells have lost their tongues.

Already the storied windows are stained
another color, empty of promise
or deliverance. His mind's a rasp,

a wheel turned against flint. It wakes
with a guttural spark: *Niggers, niggers.*
His ancient prayer flares.

—

THE PORNOGRAPHER

Anarch of the actual, mine
is the dream of Eden,

minus a bouncer at the door,
world where Botticelli breasts

rise on imagination's foam,
where unappeasable arousal

heaves in oceanic swells. Maestro
with a metronome, miniaturist

of the oversized, I am the Siren
and ship of singular desire,

the mast you lash yourself to
to hear the unhearable and not

perish, not die entirely perhaps
to the sweet flesh, the pure

matter of being, now
puddled in your hand.

—

TIME'S SQUARE

12/31/99

And so we came to swarm about
a year too soon in the passive dark

of this idea, "millennium": this womb
of all expectations. Yet how like

cinders blown aloft on the razz-
matazz of celebration

the centuries winked out and fell
unnoticed around us. And so on

through the night we ground
our way, enthronged, body

to body, thrust together,
engendering a future, tripwire

lovers all at the stroke, our confetti
like so much ignorant seed.

———

TATTOO

I've tried to keep my mind a blank
canvas while the artist's electric
fire prowls my thigh, and trust
in his expertise to affix the ink
exactly as designed—an intricate
interlocking of double, fracted
curves that should, I've planned, shift
kinetically: a fluid shadow
at the groin—abstracted, yes,
but still, one might imagine dolphins
breaking through the surface, those pirates'
souls transformed, leaping up
from the troubled sea of their denial,
attending, at last, a god in their midst.

O, Martyrs! Slowly beneath the needle's
wasping, beneath what seems random
sputterings of jet and blood (*What
have I done?*), the lines begin
to arc across my leg's pale ocean,
then coil back to their lasting deep
embrace with skin and schema. Yet why
this adolescent ritual, this whim
at forty-eight? Wasn't the sanctioned
infantile knife enough, or the chrism
and splash to the brow, the bishop's slap,
the banns and vows, the *Forgive me, Father,
for I have sinned?* I should have no need
of selfish sacrament, this stain

that casts me out. But look—it's done.

—

SONNET

Some days deep in the mind's dark,
the path trails off, and the unknown
way's the footfall of syntax through
undergrowth so dense and lush
that whatever idea spurred you on
this journey's now in parenthesis,
deletable, soon to be the smudged
erasure of your good intent,
the manifest made invisible, the world
embracing so much less, till tweezed
of all, all's this ghosted hiatus,
this gaunt nought: the pure imagined
poem, here in this wondrous place
where you cannot survive for long.

———

IN THE POEM OF SOCIAL CONSCIENCE

words the poet's nailed
to the page begin eventually

to smell like mutinous legionnaires
the emperor's ordered crucified

after long torture, yet still
they struggle in their throes,

calling out for pity, the sponge
water-sopped, whatever . . .

day after day, the desperate
syllables oddly never fainter,

lining as they do the entire
chariot-rutted Appian Way.

———

HUMMINGBIRD EXHIBIT

San Diego Animal Park

Adjusting each time to their junglized air
becomes a matter of will, a shedding of self-

consciousness, a necessary fall back to naked glee,
the kind children have at first sighting these quasi-

prelapsarian birds. There, for example, two spatting
Beryllines flare like cat's-eyes under a jeweller's loupe,

lustrous Lilliputians, too comical by half for anyone
to believe that one could indeed injure the other;

or, hearing the belle-voiced Calliopes peel by
in tiny sonic booms, an adult can't help but wonder

why the red current of a heart would want
to keep that dervish pace. It isn't joy exactly

nor awe that I feel here, but a chill at the all-too
familiar, as when a diaphanous whirr chitters

a threat before me—a Lucifer according to the wall-chart,
his throat a blaze of hellfire, slashing his scimitar bill

from side to side—asserting dominion over a red-tipped vial
of sugarwater. If I move away, he'd let me watch

the supple black lash of his tongue flick then draw
the crystal fluid out, till—clearer still—a pure sphere,

a granule of his spent breath, lofts slowly through the tube:
contentment's quiet orison at the surfeit of desire. Then *pfft*,

gone, like paradise. And yet I confess their loveliness,
the immutable urge that hammered out their brilliant mettle

at the same forge where humans fashion hell: *I need, I want,
I take*. Such a lonely vantage, this awareness that comes

from time to time among them till I find my way again
to an exit and the first thinning blast of California air.

—

INTERSECTIONS

Bib-Rambla, Granada

In the shaded square near the chapel
where the Catholic Monarchs lie encased
in black lead, beside the Mad, the Vain,
the Too-Soon-Dead, I sat among flower stalls
clustered around the fountain and thumbed
my well-worn Lonely Planet guide to plot
the next few hours' diversion. I didn't see
at first the black-garbed gypsy woman prowling
among the café tables, offering sprigs of rosemary,
tapers of remembrance. When she pinned me finally
with her kohl-darkened eyes and said she'd chart
my hand's arroyos, I let her. An amusement

costing but small change. Her callused hand
formed a nest of warm straw in which mine nestled.
As if detached, I watched her trace my past and hint
—at what? I couldn't understand her Spanish
and before I could she left to ply another corner
of the square. When I bent again to reading
I learned that in that very spot the Inquisition
used to put the wayward to the lash. Still,
arpeggios of water arced into light and scents
swirled at random from the stalls. I wanted to stay
forever in that ignorant present amid the useless
mementos we store up free of nuisance and history.

But eight streets webbed out from that plaza. Then eight
streets more, and soon I found myself along the Darro,
peering up at the balcony where Irving penned his tales
of the Alhambra—"one of the pleasantest dreams of a life,"
he claims, despite the "sterile road" of exile described

on his final page: when Boabdil, the last Moorish king
in Spain, looks back and lets escape his "infamous sigh"
toward the summit where Fernando no doubt
stood in the wake of that despair, with Isabel
resplendent in lead-black cloak and crown. Why
must I now give you only this story, though eight
streets led from that plaza, and eight streets more?

———

TOURISTS

Megalops atlanticus, Old Town, Key West

Hearty-voiced, hawking his day's catch,
he'd set a makeshift table dockside
and stood behind, still briny with sweat,
but proud and silver-haired, the serrated
steel glinting in his sun-mottled hand.
Nine tuna steaks already were arrayed
against the slick, white plank, each
medallion the lustrous ferric red of Japanese
porcelain rising through fired glaze.

The pungent guts, the hacked
gobbets of waste shimmered
as he tossed them toward pelicans
gathered below. Their splayed wings
luffed like canvas in headwind; their feet
pattered the harbor's murk to lurch
ahead with bills clacking to scoop a prize,
the dip-net of each bare pouch extended
blindly in hunger for whatever chance

might provide. What more did we want
by lingering there, shutters clicking, if not
the startling sinew of light that sliced
through clouded depths, the great circle of an eye
hard against silver armature, the near length
of a man, its pointed mouth up-turned, tearing
the surface, voracious as a god staking claim
to the very air. Not knowing what, we gasped
as if some thug had slipped a shiv between our ribs.

—

HYMN

Autumnal equinox   a tumbling field
     galactic dust   spun off from dying suns
a wedge of darkness   an axehead felling light

and yet the asters' equipoise   the bees'
     unwavering hum   a holy stasis glimpsed
before the mind ruptures on the thought

then gone and I'm back   sifting the stuttered chaff
     of loss   and love   and longing   time's
continuum strung like beads into decades

an arthritic's devotions   an effort
     year by year   (so great therefore)
what I winnow here might well be praise

—

AQUARELLE

to make of the thing at hand:
to dip from the earthen
bruised lip of the faience cup

and stain again this Arctic
you'd escape from: to touch
the sable to it till it pools

somehow into dance: to say
that split-leaf philodendron
rootbound in the corner must

pirouette with light, become
the tropic you'd inhabit, if only
for a while: such coalescing

green—you never imagined till now
this is how the hard-white ground
you left untouched from the start

would insist on bursting through.

—

WHAT WAS GIVEN

What was given came without
the usual reasons—the earth

that day having completed
no meaningful circuit of the sun.

The giving should have been cause enough
for surprise, or that hidden beneath

patterned folds of wrap, within
a box large as any man's bewilderment,

waited some unknown thing, purchased
after long labor. How undeserved,

that unreciprocated moment,
when all the twisted paths

they'd walked together and alone,
seemed to brighten at the first tug

on the bow, the paper hinging out
like doors, the lid ready to come undone

as one stood there, still
too frightened to peer inside.

—

II. The Knot

The ashes of his fathers sprouted in his grizzled
*   beard*
Thus he carried all his heredity in his face
—Apollinaire

THE SON HE NEVER HAD

Here's to the son I never had,
my father piped one Christmas Eve

to toast a new apprentice, Tom,
my friend. Stunned red as holly

more from embarrassment
than from the schnapps they'd drunk

since quitting time, still he gulped
the liquor down, and I too

swallowed the fiery shot to ease me
closer, I supposed, to some oblivion

of my own making, while that smiling man
between us poured yet another round

and my mother, in the far remove
of her kitchen, checking the roast, declared

it done. —Some nights, feeling my favorite
cordial begin to smolder in the pit

of my stomach, it's him I summon
like a coal I thought long spent

but somehow fan to sputtering life:
I can't deny that slight, but carry it,

a father's gift, howsoever
thoughtless, lodged inside

a fertile space, engendering this
unorphaned brood of words.

—

DOUBLE GOING

Fists

Photo of my father as a boxer, ca. 1929

Ah, the impenetrable knot.
How the radiant star
of each hand has collapsed
to a brown core. Snub-
nosed mambas long
as his arms. Surrogate cocks,
his cowries, his charms. Shrunken
skulls with lips and eyes
sewn fast. How mute
yet mocking, these amputees
swaggering their bald huzzahs

before the world. I'm twice
what he was there, the stunning
gesture punctuating
the decades before my birth,
the blue contusion back-
lighting my sisters' Bronx,
then mine. Punch, parry,
counterpunch—he's
dead—yet still these clenched
fists, these mallets gaveling
against the planks of heaven.

Toolbox

What to make of this wicked
legacy: your clutch
of crick-necked nails; the sac
of screws stripped by your hand's
unyielding torque; the scarred,
blunted steels—these totems
of your craft, unsaintly martyr's
attributes you couldn't sell

or bear to keep. I wince
to see the care you took
to arrange this gift, how
you must have raised each item
to scrutiny, judged it fit

to give a son to puzzle
out a use. Practical
need makes me bend
these many years after
to sift the shrapnel of your love
for one uncrimped helix,
just one uncrippled shaft
I can turn or hammer home.

Waltz

Some days I'm not willing to share
this music's triple shimmer,
this Danube cascade that floods
my living room, nor grant him
a soul, dancing, spun
like flax into thread, nor imagine
him fleshed again, suited
at his daughter's wedding, her veil
a comet blazoned with
the trajectory of his pride.

But the cadence swells each time,
and I cry to capture him,
fleeting across the years'
icy vacuum, twirled
into lusty, joyous being
here—unwelcome revenant—
lightfooting his way beyond
the measured bars, even
as the after-echo
plunges on toward silence.

Smokes

I've tried to shake the habit,
but keep coaxing the dust-
blue poison of you
out of the air's oblivion
until from deep in my lungs
the sweet, palpable release
swirls through the house.

A shock of sperm defining
every cell, a stream
of milk, sophistication's
brief pretense ending—
where?—with this faltering ash.

So why the addictive love/
hate, this holy office
I repeat from one stale
room to the next? My words
hover about me with gray
detachment, and yet each breath's
freighted with your ghost.

Solder

Memory: the acetylene
hiss. The flinty snap
at a squeeze of his hand. A surg-
ical spike of Prussian blue
wielded like a priest-
king's flail. The heavy iron's
red admonishment
as he tried to teach me, twelve,
his fearsome mysteries.

The unalloyed disaster
that I was brazed his eyes:
Each soft spooled thread
of leaded tin I touched
with that brand pooled at the tip
and fell, wasted to the floor.
Look! and I did, down
to where my feet had fused
in a sky of jagged stars.

Eggs

So few, the rotten ones,
their brimstone stench smoothly
encalcified in icelight
till I knock and it's opened
to me—the air suddenly
fouled, and fear again
cradled cozily in my palm:

If ever I hear ya got
a girl pregnant, I'll crush
yer balls like pigeon eggs.

Ravenous, cantankered
Cronus, am I the stone,
the shape that swelled your gut,
the oracular seed that split
and grew beyond perfection—
the germ, the progeny
you vomited into life?

Fishline

Wondrous, how his thumb's
steady brake unreeled
that taut, translucid nerve
as it sped plumb-straight
to the deep while a whir rose
from the callus like a song.
But always then the abrasion
of disappointment: his laugh

at my burning palm as the line
raced beyond control
till a useless thicket brambled
from the spool. Yet now that hand
feeds this other filament—
as thin, perdurable, and blue—
and sets its baited lure
trawling the papery lights.

Mirror

Stepping from the shower,
I find you scrimmed, deep
within that simpler dimension,
peering through cataracts
directly out at me.

Is it my future, this
distortion, or merely the haunting
past, or what sense tells me:
the palpable divide
between flesh and ash.

O, to erase every
last aspect of you
with one overarching gesture
and stand for once in clarity,
naked and wholly alone.

Garden

Tilled and mulched with fish
guts and horse manure
hauled from a millionaire's stable,
his penny-parcel square
of rented land burgeoned
each spring with bite and grit:
radish, spinach, kale.

Such bitterness crowded
our silent table. *Essen,*
nicht fressen! But dumb
as a calf raised at a trough,
I sat and cleared my plate,
then mouthed the difficult grace,
missing the means to praise.

Scotch

Now the ice chimes in
the hours of forgetting—smoky
gemlight, bewitching cupola,
the first fiery kiss—
a god's annunciation.

Do I speak in tongues?
You must have staggered too
toward this revelation's blaze.

The truth chinks and hisses
gently in the glass,
and what you slurred to the darkened
world was gone by morning:
I'm not my father's son.

Alba

The thought grinds against
thought, improbable brew:
he, an Italian in silk,
the Forum choked with the rush-
hour, waspish buzz of Rome.
Yet love was there. —My eyes

open on layered heights,
twinned histories—petty
and imperial: He strode
beside me, barrel-chested
at forty-six, his voice
intimate, like leaves at dawn.

Shucking

It became your flamenco, each
theatrical plunge to heft
a sea-tight castanet
from the brimming pail, then flourish

the knife an instant before
swiftly cleaving the shells.
I watched you watch me gulp

that salty flesh, like phlegm.
So many little deaths
I survived before I learned
to relish what you'd killed.

Cremains

Gone?—the blood, the bile,
the dark humors, spit,
piss, snot, bellowed
breath, his rare remorse-
less tears. So what is here:

pumice . . . a pure Arizona—
my heart's dry domain.
I sift, I till, for what?
A root, a sprout, but still
the fathers I create remain.

Pocketwatch

This keepsake of final partings
tsk-tsks through all
my hours, yet daily I ratchet

its springs to the limit and let
myself be pulled in the relent-
less wake of your passage: you,

Valentino-slick, yet hard
by the gunwale in '28,
the present clamped in your hand.

Swing

I arced higher each time,
fearless from the thrust of his arms
till the weighted world turvied
beneath me. How could he

have known his giddy, pinioned
boy, beyond his care-
less reach, would never fall
but once from that sea-deep sky?

Barrow

Its tethered, clackety dance
had set the cobbles knocking.
A nervous tattoo. When the butcher

gunned a rivet through

its skull, my head squirmed
in your palms' insistent vise:
This'll make a man of you.

Kodaks

Each word's an aperture
I let him enter by;
each poem, a negative

coddled through cold acid
baths, my mind's blooded
lights: *I* give him life.

Whittle

To slice the blade clean
through the sapling branch
unflinchingly thumbward—
Trust me—I doubt I dared
to learn, but can see you still

among those flowering crabs
sliding the bark's slick
sheath partway from the core,
then notching it, a deft flick

here, and there, testing
it first with your lips, a one-
note whistle for your boy:

a grace note, surely, now
grown necessary, held

in the mind, my diapason.

—

III. Retrievals

To see clearly at a distance
To see everything
Near at hand
            —Apollinaire

LYRIC

I'm tired too of this rusty anvil
on which I've tried to hammer out

a soul's thin foil. It's become
a stubby pedestal for the forgettable

man's effigy, a generic glyph
interrupting every hero's frieze.

Some days it's been a perch for vultures,
an altar to sacrifice a childhood on

in hope of grace. Or it's the ego's
phallus straining toward a sky,

when *you* would be a better well
to pump. Now here it is strutting,

a thin scar borne like a badge
on a Prussian's cheek, or here a pillar

of salt weeping in desert wind,
but most nights it's still the tiny

tragedian, mad and blind,
a familiar representative

sending *ai*'s echoing among
the rafters, where I find myself

from time to time slumped in the cheap
last row, mouthing back the lines.

—

AN ABIDING

The day the x-ray showed your lung ghost-laced
with fluid, a carrier pigeon came to rest
in the small delta of the woodland garden
we'd wedged against the forest, and forage awhile
beneath the hanging feeder and ornamentals
we'd hoped might thrive for years in dappling seep-
ages of summer light: A pure extreme,
a white so milk-souled only its eyes' black
beads and an azure ring on its left foot
seemed to wed it to this world. A cipher,
from where, for whom, whose paraclete
nearly fearless as we peered from the living
room window? Each thread of reason frayed
and snapped with unbearable possibilities.
All that week—in the limbo of waiting, as
we learned the arcanum of disease, its likely
crabwise crawl through ever-deepening burrows,
thinking to prepare for the worst will make
it easier when it comes—there in the garden
that stark and wayward mystery lingered among
the blood-red rhododendrons, and when we knew
finally, we saw from the shadowed window
where we stood in long embrace, trembling,
the bird was gone, and all around would be
as it had been, for better or for worse.

—

GARDEN SPIDER

Argiope bruennichi

An orbweaver, adrift among
the hosta's spent stalks, black
and brilliant-banded gold, dead-

center in a mist of silks and two
zigzag vertical rays strung as luminous
warning to any flying bird, hovered

last evening, head earthward, her legs
poised to set the web trembling to a blur
each time I crouched to watch, spell-

bound and snared with the thought
that here's the perfect fretwork
to grace a backyard garden. Now

this morning I see she's consumed
each filament, digested the indispensible
proteins to respin the entire design

somewhere away from my quisitive gaze.
What must I admire, left with empty
space: an unbending mind

fixed on private workings, or the way
the very fabric of a world
can be chewed up for weaving again?

—

GARAGE SALE MIRROR

Where the silver backing's peeled away,
absence blooms upon its surface.
A pale impetigo now stipples the face

of the settled room, or take a step and an algae
film seems to have floated from the depth
of a shadowed stream-fed pond.

No longer amenable to what's found
in the world, but weary, it's cast a dose of epsom
in the bath, letting the salt of loss turn opalescent.

Like a damaged plate, it bears the pentimento
of past exposures, yet makes of deminishment
the ample art of capturing less.

Each image posed for its appraisal,
though it seems blottered, tarnished, misted
with decay, is flecked like schist,

a mica-sheen of the splintered day,
or etched with finger-whorls crackling
across the skin, or the almost-touch

of a ghostly brutal hand still clutching
at any unshakable light that flickers back.
Where the foil has ruptured, the long hidden rises

earth-hued from behind: a warped plank
that nonetheless keeps what shimmers anchored
in the frame. Even the casual passing eye's

jolted to glimpse the present so refracted
as through spilled oil. Yet, how luminous:
because of what is ruined, the room

brims all the more, resilvered by this lack.

———

TIRESIAS AT EVENING

How can I say it plainly: such knowledge
at first is never wisdom, but waking

as if in a strange, troughed bed to a shock of
sunlight that almost blinds, to the frantic

trill of a warbler that makes no seeming
sense: What I found missing suddenly

was something found, a fumbling
after the memory of what I was, but

was not now. A rare sensation:
I'd become the cave of my own unknowing,

and cried for the lost, hard half I
thought had kept me whole. In the mirror

my razor still crafted the usual face, my
voice still echoed with the familiar

registers of work, but I could not stand
(you laugh!) in the arena of men,

nor boast of what they'd see as shame.
Accursed, blood-driven vessels—both. Was I

doubly less or more for this (now that I can speak
as a man) this gift? They can never know—

nor you—except you open to these words and feel
each syllable thrust inside your hidden self.

———

WORK

High in August's canopy
among their still-green
bounty, squirrels
are early-harvesting.
They ply each limb—
deft, rasp-toothed
severers—till acorns
plummet, so many
relief packages thudding
through quiet leaves
at the garden's border.

My dog senses the futility
of lofty awareness,
though his ears twitch
even in the drowse
of his contentment beside me.
My morning coffee grows cold.
I've let the words I was reading
scatter like finches to the oaktops.
Already the need has come
to scratch the underbrush
for sustenance.

—

ST. FRANCIS, DISTRACTED BY BIRDS

For all it matters to them, he's stone, an outsized gnome
someone's propped in the garden as a joke. They roam

the underbrush for grubs or swoop at hapless bugs
in the busy air while he sits like a rusted lug

on a wheel gone flat, the pen stalled in his fist.
Amid their trills and chirps, he's the soloist

who's flubbed his cue. The lilt of his syllables has wilted;
the rhythm's eroded; syntax snarled; the meter stilted.

To them, *tant mieux*, a truce—but on their terms: One stir
in his seat and they'll loft for cover. Blankly, he concurs . . .

and waits, becalmed within the momentary slant
of morning, its linear thrust smoothed, undulant,

bending to a curve, an everpresence flurried
with routine: a march of robins on the lawn, the hurried

combobulations of a wren, the purple finch's tread,
a brief, so brief shudder of generation wed

to extinction of self. He starts; they flee, but still the fermata
of a song shafts through the trees, fiery as stigmata.

———

SEA DUCKS IN WINTER

Was it shelter they found
there, this solstice dusk:
the narrow bay, its burnished
bituminous sheen, which
their down-ruddered feet
disturbed a moment with a dozen
delicate V's soon smudged
to settled calm: a small flotilla
of scaups and eiders rafting,
dropping anchor, twelve dark
stones dissolving upon

a rock-strewn shore—yet now
moonlight sifts through
blinds I thought I'd pulleyed
tight just hours before against
the season, so many lids willed
shut, the frayed ropes of being
intent on sleep, but mind-
ful somehow still of witness,
the night's drift, the cracks
of sound as the ducks take wing,
their sudden shadows' passing.

—

LAKE WINNIPESAUKEE

I suspect it would be easier to have the end of things
we misconceive about the world come on apocalyptic hooves—
as my good Jehovan neighbor claims from time to time,
brandishing her dogeared Revelation at my door. Surely
it would surge like a thunderhead through a gap
atop the mountain ridge, changing the day forever, and not
just appear by chance, drifting beneath summer's ordinary blue,
in the low lap of the lakeside where I was wading the shallows,
staring at nothing in particular: a mere discarded rag
that caught my eye. When I nudged it with my foot, the scrap

scattered to a thousand parts, barbeled and black-finned,
a hatch of spawn, yet there in that rippled light more
like a ruined blossom, each petal vibrant with fear,
but schooled somehow to seek survival camouflaged
as something dead, or, more cunning yet, deadly:
a pulsing sea anemone. So standing ankle-deep, I watched
the spent flower rebud itself. Its tightening drew me nearer
till, in the corner of my eye, I saw from the depths
a foot-long fish zero in. Blunt-headed, unrelenting,
primitive instinct made me jump ashore.

A catfish, whiskers twitching, probed ever closer
toward the brood. Poor mice, I thought. But then the bud
unfurled again, like arms outstretched in greeting—
and enveloped the mother. She disappeared within
her swarm of hatchlings. A hook-flash snared me,
the rusty barb of providential signs. How could I not
but try to read what seemed so clearly written there
on the water before a moment later all of it drifted—
no, aimed itself singlemindedly away—toward safety—
how could there be?—in that darkness beyond my sight.

LEAFY SEA DRAGONS AT THE MUSÉE OCÉANOGRAPHIQUE, MONACO

Phycodurus Eques

Hard to imagine their awkward dazzle
evolving, ganglia branching from nubs
of protosentient matter, into these
brittle-seeming denizens. Easier

to think a child concocted them
from balsa sticks and scissored crepe
she'd crayoned wilted lettuce-green,
and so set them dangling before us

in this watery air, ungainly puppets
strung as from an unseen hand
—except for the certain semblance
of their underlying shape to the sun-

devouring, slash-clawed beast
that slithers from the human cave
to embroid in time the tyrant's gown
of flame. What mystic first dreamt them

adrift and potent among otherworldly reefs?—
so unlike these pale, imperiled offspring
of the planet's dawn, which we cloister
here, as if the vital need were theirs alone.

—

AT THE CATHÉDRALE STE-RÉPARATE

Nice

Beneath the dome's emerald glaze, within
its shaded refuge where sifted lights angled down
from the cupola's lantern windows, dusting the slabbed,
empty nave . . . among its baroque pastels and gilt,
despite the soothing quiet undisturbed
but for my footsteps . . . I felt no God

residing there. My coins in the votive box clanked
like chains; still I lit a candle to the patron saint:
virgin intermediary, martyred at fifteen, her corpse
uncorrupted and set adrift in a bark of flowers.
What extremes of innocence harnessed the winged
angels who towed that sea-tossed vessel here?

I'd rather have laughed at the tone-deaf bishop who denied
Paganini a funeral in that space, believing
him the devil incarnate for the sounds that flamed
from his violin, howling like witches'
familiars, each string a cat in heat, unsettling
the Catholic quiet of summer nights in Nice.

But in their crimson cups that day, small fires
danced on molten seas. This is the brink we set
prayers sailing on, across infinite silence
till one by one they flicker out in tiny gasps
of smoke. This is what I did by custom
or necessity, only half-expecting answers.

So when I heard tapping on the floor and turned
to see a stray dog loping, tail held high, altar
to altar in shaggy ecstasy, ears tuned in
to unhearable music, a frequency beyond
range, it was no mongrel sacrilege I sensed.
I felt my pulse in each echo of his paws.

—

MONKS TOURING THE PAPAL PALACE

Avignon

Moving quickly through the vaulted
halls, austere and bone-chilling
in winter as any meat locker,
I can only imagine the pontifical
opulence that once reigned here—
the thought itself almost in schism
with common Christian sense—
until I'm suddenly stalled
in the popes' bed chamber,
in the midst of a dozen barely
postpubescent boys, black-coped
and tonsured like their elder
chaperones—so that I begin
futilely summoning the ABC's
of sanctity: Augustinian, Benedictine,
Cistercian?—all of us one dark flock
for the moment staring at the lavish,
reconstructed murals: delicate
gold vines tendriling through night-
blue skies, morphing into hierarchies
of crosiers begetting smaller crosiers,
the whole projected dream a calming
seamless net cast upon the papal sea.
What must they think, standing here
like cast iron bells, the slender tongues
of their bodies hidden within? What peal
reverberates? From across the room,
I'm struck by the rose-cold face and hands
of one boy, who, for such exposure,
might well have graced a Caravaggio
except for his cropped, boot-camp

hair and black ungainly halo, worn
a size too large, it seems, and slipped
down to his ears. And yet, alone,
I might attempt, corruptingly,
here, to kiss him on the lips, still
cupid-bowed, agape, and raised in wonder.

—

GLASS

Verrerie du Vieux Moulin, Biot

The way he holds the hollow
six-foot tube with its bulb
of molten glass glowing at the tip,

he might be Gabriel, his cheeks
ballooned, prefiguring the coming
change, for surely it's angelic how

corruptible breath can swell
the globe toward beauty, how dust
of metal oxides become incarnate,

coloring the hidden design
from the start: that the dull
antimony powder, in which he rolls

the orb, will flame to solar
yellows, and the manganese
gem itself as amethyst, but more

akin to the miraculous, that white
river-pebbles, calcined and crushed,
when mixed with the potash

of burnt seaweed can melt
in the furnace core to spirit-
water clarity. His art's in teasing

the still soft mass with a pontil,
pinching, prodding, collapsing
the glob, until with a deft twirl

of the iron rod, all suddenly
devolves like a morning
glory bud, fanning open

into wordless expression, a vessel
born blistering, that the mind's
fingers craved to hold.

—

SWIMMER AT THE Y

Within his adopted element, skin sealed
to fluid otherness, he's muscled light,

a lithe Proteus, now otter-sleek, now oiled
machine pistoning through a stroke

while I, clamped fast in the vise
of a chlorinated wheeze, sit slug-

pale at poolside, syncopating each breath
by half to the steady fluttered rhythm

of his legs and, yes, envying how the barely
spandexed swath of his behind jackknifes

at each lap into unrefracted clarity
before he sinks, then springs torpedo-

rigid from the turn to surface through rippling
sheaths of glass, all sinewed geometry,

rhomboids and trapezius shifting
with measured angularity, his mind,

entire in the flesh, unthrottled now—
as mine—wholly toward this motion.

—

HOME AFTER MONTHS AWAY

for Donald Perret

Now the bags you lugged past Customs lie
exposed across the bed, exhaling their last
breaths scented with the places you've been.

Now the maps you've piled atop the bureau,
recreased a hundred times and torn (whole
cities gone), slowly collapse like an old

accordion wheezing closed on melodies,
yet despite the furniture hazed with dust, the tomb-
stale air, this homely destination

hugs you lover-tight, having grown
vaguely unfamiliar, odd, yet freshened
for being so. Soon you'll search the rooms

to relocate forgotten trifles. Your quotidian
knife and fork you'll discover among the usual
clutter of the kitchen drawer. You'll eat

this meal alone, exhausted with journey, content
with the simple but spiced aromas swirling
from the stove. Your dinner plate with its crizzled

glaze will suddenly seem patterned in a way
you never noticed before: the border etched
with winged serpents, a cartographer's

device, framing a dim, amazed reflection
of your face—the terra incognita
that never felt like home till now.

A BOTTLE OF CHÂTEAU D'YQUEM 1966

I cannot speak of any perfect balance
between the wine's color and the tannin of the cask,

or even whether some lusciousness adhered
anywhere else than to the glasses we raised

in toasts to our lives and all the sentiments
we thought that extravagant wine embodied, nor,

today, could I swear it held the promised hint
of ripened apricots or pears. I'd like

to believe whatever substance passed across
our tongues became the body's, could not be forgotten,

not become the mere evaporate we shared,
leaving no residue other than abstractions,

not leave us empty. When you told me
you'd saved the bottle all these years, I asked,

What for? Now you write that cancer grips
you like a weasel at the throat, that surgeons

have cut away part of your tongue and palate.
My encouragements sputter, seem like dregs.

Even this poem, which emerged from the pale citrine
of my writing tablet, lets a sediment escape:

If only you'd . . . You shouldn't've. This
is the radiation of reason, the chemo of acceptance:

that the anarchic cell's secure in the fortress
of the world's marrow. And yet tonight,

wandering the garden, shuddering beneath the chill
sepulchral light of the Paschal moon,

I saw the jonquils bent again in the mythic
posture of the self-absorbed, so many

silent mouths turned toward the grub-laden
earth. But how that narrow band of yellow

thrust against the overarching night:
a glow, defiant, as if willed, though brief—

Château d'Yquem, I whispered. *Château d'Yquem*.

———

SNAKESKIN

In the first shock of finding it so casually
draped like a tulle scarf among
the headboard's spiked acanthus,
we felt certain it hadn't been there
the evening before as we stripped
by candlelight in the ancient farmhouse
to canter through the long winter night
atop the broad back of a horsehair
mattress, but then in late morning's cold,
sun shafting across the counterpane
where our bodies huddled, twined
as much in fear as against the chill
of wondering where the living sinew
lurked—close, we thought, to the radiant
warmth of chest to back, cock nuzzled
to cleft—that castoff sheath seemed kin
to our desire, a brittle casing, the ghosted
flesh grown firm again only in imagination,
so fragile in that light, like spun confection,
or the vellum scroll whereon is writ
(if we'd but tried to read it then) the forgotten
formula for love's replenishment.

—

FATHER'S DAY IN PALMYRA, NY

for Thom and Barbara Ward

Over the next hill, a golden angel, I'm told,
descended in 1823, but here, beyond
this lawn where four generations have gathered
to honor the fathers yet among them, I prefer

the solace of the practical field of winter wheat
ready for mowing. I sit through the late
spring day, a stranger to most in the family—
fatherless, childless, a guest not quite

at ease. At the lawn's edge, as if to interrupt
my attempts at conversation, an oriole
is striking clear crystal high in a cottonwood,
a bel canto chimed insistently.

I squint awhile, up to where the wind
lifts the hearty leaves, and catch
no glimpse of orange yellow. I see
instead the leaves paddling like the fans

of a thousand maiden aunts as the air
suddenly fills with a squall of seeds,
like the feathered aftermath of nephews
pillow-fighting with friends. Lost above

me somewhere, the oriole still repeats
his aria, oddly unperturbed by this snow
that's fallen around us and the human
laughter drifting up over the field and hill.

———

ACKNOWLEDGMENTS

I wish to thank the editors of the following publications in which these poems, some in earlier versions, appeared:

Beloit Poetry Journal: "Church Burning," "Fog," "Insects at Night," "Petit Mal";

The Blue Moon Review: "What Was Given";

Boulevard: "Aquarelle" (as "Vichy Matisse"), "Fists," "Hummingbird Exhibit," "Tourette's";

Center: A Journal of the Literary Arts: "Wisteria";

Cider Press Review: "Leafy Sea Dragons at the Musée Océanographique, Monaco";

Connecticut Review: "Solder";

The Cortland Review: "The Pornographer," "Tattoo";

Island (Australia): "Garden Spider";

Kestrel: "Alba," "Barrow," "Cremains," "Eggs," "Kodaks," "Shucking," "Swing," "Whittle";

Literal Latté: "At the Cathédrale Ste-Réparate";

Maine Times: "Photograph of Angela, 1929," "Sea Ducks in Winter," "The Weight of the Past";

Mid-American Review: "Lake Winnipesaukee";

The Nebraska Review: "Glass";

New England Review: "The Lighthouse at Cassis," "Peonies";

North American Review: "Toolbox," "Waltz";

Pleiades: "Intersections," "In the Poem of Social Conscience";

Poet Lore: "Monks Touring the Papal Palace," "Time's Square," "Work";

Poetry: "Father's Day in Palmyra, NY," "Fishline," "Garden," "Mirror," "Pocketwatch," "Scotch";

Prairie Schooner: "An Abiding," "Tourists";

Reed Magazine: "The Lost," "St. Francis, Distracted by Birds";

Southwest Review: "A Bottle of Château d'Yquem 1966";

Sundog: "Tantum Ergo";

Tar River Poetry: "Garage Sale Mirror," "Swimmer at the Y";

The Texas Review: "Anna's House," "Grand Mal," "Home After Months Away," "Hymn";

TriQuarterly: "Snakeskin," "Sonnet."

"Tiresias at Evening" first appeared in the anthology *Chick for a Day*, edited by Fiona Giles (Simon & Schuster, 2000).

I am grateful to the Maine Arts Commission for a 1997 Individual Artist Fellowship that assisted me financially during the writing of this book. I also wish to thank the Corporation of Yaddo, the Fundación Valparaíso, the Gell Center, and the Camargo Foundation for providing me with the creative solitude in which many of these poems were written.

———

ABOUT THE AUTHOR

Richard Foerster was born in the Bronx, New York, and attended Fordham University and the University of Virginia. He is the author of three previous collections, *Sudden Harbor* and *Patterns of Descent* (both published by Orchises Press) and *Trillium* (BOA Editions, 1998), which received Honorable Mention for the 2000 Poets' Prize. Other honors include the "Discovery"/*The Nation* Award, *Poetry* magazine's Bess Hokin Prize, fellowships from the National Endowment for the Arts and the Maine Arts Commission, and the 2000/2001 Amy Lowell Poetry Travelling Scholarship. He has worked as a lexicographer, educational writer, typesetter, and as the editor of the literary magazine *Chelsea*. He currently lives in York Beach, Maine.

—

BOA EDITIONS, LTD.
AMERICAN POETS CONTINUUM SERIES

No. 1   *The Fuhrer Bunker: A Cycle
of Poems in Progress*
W. D. Snodgrass

No. 2   *She*
M. L. Rosenthal

No. 3   *Living With Distance*
Ralph J. Mills, Jr.

No. 4   *Not Just Any Death*
Michael Waters

No. 5   *That Was Then: New and
Selected Poems*
Isabella Gardner

No. 6   *Things That Happen Where
There Aren't Any People*
William Stafford

No. 7   *The Bridge of Change:
Poems 1974–1980*
John Logan

No. 8   *Signatures*
Joseph Stroud

No. 9   *People Live Here: Selected
Poems 1949–1983*
Louis Simpson

No. 10 *Yin*
Carolyn Kizer

No. 11 *Duhamel: Ideas of Order in
Little Canada*
Bill Tremblay

No. 12 *Seeing It Was So*
Anthony Piccione

No. 13 *Hyam Plutzik: The Collected
Poems*

No. 14 *Good Woman: Poems and a
Memoir 1969–1980*
Lucille Clifton

No. 15 *Next: New Poems*
Lucille Clifton

No. 16 *Roxa: Voices of the Culver
Family*
William B. Patrick

No. 17 *John Logan: The Collected Poems*

No. 18 *Isabella Gardner: The
Collected Poems*

No. 19 *The Sunken Lightship*
Peter Makuck

No. 20 *The City in Which I Love You*
Li-Young Lee

No. 21 *Quilting: Poems 1987–1990*
Lucille Clifton

No. 22 *John Logan: The Collected
Fiction*

No. 23 *Shenandoah and Other Verse
Plays*
Delmore Schwartz

No. 24 *Nobody Lives on Arthur
Godfrey Boulevard*
Gerald Costanzo

No. 25 *The Book of Names: New and
Selected Poems*
Barton Sutter

No. 26 *Each in His Season*
W. D. Snodgrass

No. 27 *Wordworks: Poems Selected
and New*
Richard Kostelanetz

No. 28 *What We Carry*
Dorianne Laux

No. 29 *Red Suitcase*
Naomi Shihab Nye

No. 30 *Song*
Brigit Pegeen Kelly

No. 31 *The Fuehrer Bunker:
The Complete Cycle*
W. D. Snodgrass

No. 32 *For the Kingdom*
Anthony Piccione

No. 33 *The Quicken Tree*
Bill Knott

No. 34 *These Upraised Hands*
William B. Patrick

No. 35 *Crazy Horse in Stillness*
William Heyen